Mazie's Amazing Journey

From Immigrant to U.S. Senator

By Leslie Ann Hayashi
Illustrated by Tammy Yee

In honor of sweet Caroline Smith,
who was the best mother and friend a daughter could ever have.

Mary Smith, President, American Bar Association (2023-2024)

JAPAN

Fukushima

Yokohama

PACIFIC OCEAN

28 27 26 25 24   5 4 3 2 1

ISBN 978-1-63905-557-9

www.shopABA.org

While running for American Bar Association president as the first Native American woman, some questioned whether I fit the image of such a leader. That led me to ask the question, "What does a lawyer look like?" Then I realized that we needed to inspire children of color to become lawyers, judges, politicians, and even presidents of the American Bar Association regardless of how they look. It is my hope this series will do just that.

Mary Smith
President, American Bar Association (2023-2024)

USS President Cleveland

THE
HAWAIIAN ISLANDS

Wave after wave broke against the *USS President Cleveland* as the ship plowed through the indigo sea. Below deck, eight-year-old Keiko moaned. Her mother dabbed her forehead with a cool towel, murmuring, "The seasickness will soon pass."

Soon Keiko's seasickness turned into homesickness. She pictured her beloved grandmother standing on the dock waving goodbye to her. "*Baachan*, I miss you," cried Keiko. *Oh, what will happen to me?*

Keiko could not know that her mother's decision to leave Japan and live in Hawai`i would shape her mind and heart. She would become a woman full of compassion and strength, proudly serving Hawai`i's people as a lawyer, legislator, lieutenant governor, and later in the US Congress.

New beginnings required a new name. After docking in
Honolulu Harbor and finding a tiny room in a boarding house,
mother Laura turned to her oldest son, "You are Roy and Keiko,
you are Mazie. And Shigeki will be Wayne when *Baachan* and *Jiichan*
bring him in a few years."

Like the trees in the autumn back home, the Hirono family began shedding
their past to embrace the ways of their new country.

Laura found a job as a typesetter with a Japanese newspaper company but the pay was low, forcing her to take a second job with a lu`au caterer.

Working late and into the early morning hours, Laura barely had enough time to change clothes and get to her day job, which left Mazie and Roy free to roam through the neighborhood, climb trees, and stay out late.

At school, Mazie struggled to blend in. Although she looked like many of her classmates, Mazie felt different. She didn't speak English and she came to school barefoot while others wore shoes or rubber slippers. She had to adjust to cafeteria food—milk in waxy cartons, apples, and white bread smeared with butter. Mazie found it easier to remain quiet and observe as thoughts constantly swirled in her head.

Every so often, Mother would add a dime to their school lunch money, which Roy would spend while Mazie tucked hers away in a worn baseball-tin shaped piggy bank that Mother had given her. Sometimes she would shake the bank to hear the reassuring sounds of the coins clinking against each other. Other nights she would lay out the dimes in rows, counting them, which made her feel safe.

One day Mazie reached for her piggy bank. No clinking sounds. Not a single coin rattled inside. It was completely empty. Before she could ask what happened to her beloved coins, her mother appeared.

"I'm sorry but I had to buy food," she apologized. "I'm sorry."

Mazie bit her lip. There was nothing to do but start over, just like coming to Hawai`i. Start over and hope for a better life.

From that day on, Mazie began saving every cent she could. Both children pitched in. After school Roy delivered newspapers and stocked shelves at a supermarket and Mazie, too, delivered newspapers.

In the meantime, Mazie studied hard at school. One of her favorite places was the library, where she helped sort and shelve books before school started. This quiet world of books became Mazie's haven—a place to dream, to grow, and to learn. Miss Petrie, the school librarian, recommended various books and now Mazie was never without a book—reading while cooking dinner, washing dishes, walking to school, and on the weekends perched in the nearby jacaranda tree. Words whisked Mazie away to worlds she had never imagined.

Soon Mazie's love of reading kindled a love of writing. Vivid descriptions inspired her to create her own images. When a teacher praised her writing, Mazie realized she too could make words sing on paper.

The more Mazie embraced a love of learning, the more she wanted to continue her studies. Although finances were still a struggle, Mazie became the first in the family to attend college. Now textbooks became her constant companion.

On campus, Mazie watched college students protesting an unpopular war. Several of her friends became active in politics hoping to change the world. Others went to law school before running for office. Inspired, Mazie decided she too would need a law degree to make a difference, and she set her heart on attending school far away from home.

In law school, as Mazie read case books filled with stories of people who went to court, she learned to think like a lawyer—to analyze, reason, and think logically. She came to understand how certain words helped while others harmed individuals and communities. Learning about the law and legal system instilled in her a desire to help others. As an immigrant and having grown up poor, Mazie felt a special responsibility to those like her.

Most of her life, Mazie had been quiet and reserved. Content to work behind the scenes, she had managed political campaigns for others. But if she was truly going to give a voice to her ideas, it was time to run for office herself. Rarely had Mazie spoken to large crowds but now she stood before microphones to rally her supporters. Mazie also went door to door, listening to the voters. Laura and *Baachan* worked hard on her campaigns and Mazie won several races.

As a lawyer-legislator, Mazie introduced laws that would make sweeping changes. This was the way to help all those who had no voice, like the at-risk youth she had spent a summer trying to help; workers like her mother who couldn't afford health insurance; and others who had no one to fight for them.

One of Mazie's elementary school classmates never had money for school lunch. It was his face that Mazie saw when she introduced a bill to provide free lunches in all public schools. No child should ever go hungry.

And it was the memory of her mother and grandmother crying as they sat beside her baby sister Yuriko. With no money for medical care, Yuriko died of pneumonia. The thought of her sister's ashes in the urn in the hotokesama, the family shrine, made Mazie fight for free medical care for all. No one should die because they couldn't afford medical care.

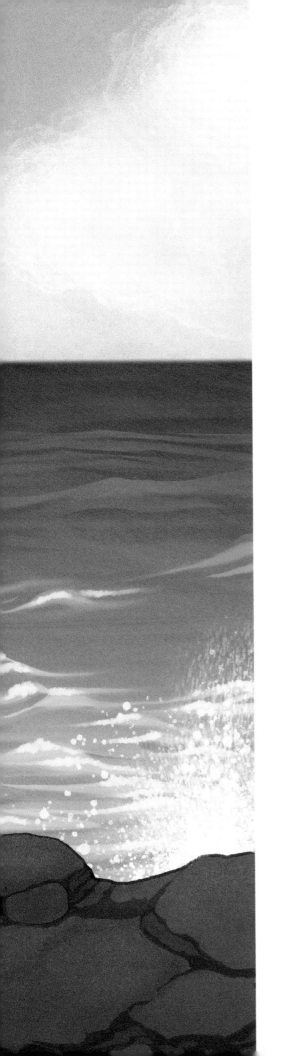

Later, when immigrant children and parents were separated at the borders, Mazie's heart broke, remembering her younger brother, Wayne. He never recovered from his early separation, struggling in school and all through his short life. His only joy was fishing from the shoreline near their home until a large wave swept him into the ocean at the age of twenty-six. No family should suffer the pain of separation, and Mazie vowed to do everything to keep parents and children together.

Mazie chose her own path, inspired by her mother who met each challenge that came her way without fear or hesitation. And with her lawyer skills, she became the first female senator from Hawai`i; the only immigrant senator currently serving; the first Buddhist senator; and the first Asian American woman elected to the U.S. Senate.

And now with a stroke of her pen, Mazie could choose words that would protect, provide, and allow others to dream big.

SENATOR HIRONO

Mazie Hirono

Important Dates

November 3, 1947	Born in Fukushima, Japan, to Matabe and Chieko (Sato) Hirono; named Keiko, which means "celebrated child"
1950	One-year-old sister Yuriko dies of pneumonia
	Chieko makes plans to leave her abusive husband and return to Hawai`i; she had been born there and lived there for the first fifteen years of her life, calling herself Laura
March 11, 1955	Arrives in Honolulu sailing aboard the *USS President Cleveland* with her mother and older brother; her younger brother and grandparents arrive a few years later
	Laura gives new names to her children; Roy for older brother Yoshikazu, Mazie for Keiko, and Wayne for younger brother Shigeki
August 21, 1959	Hawai`i becomes the 50th state
October 22, 1959	Laura, Roy, Mazie, and Wayne become naturalized citizens
1970	Graduates Phi Beta Kappa from the University of Hawai`i at Manoa with a B.A. in Psychology

March 24, 1978	Wayne, younger brother, drowns while shoreline fishing
May 1978	Receives law degree from Georgetown University Law Center in Washington, D.C.
	Is admitted to the Hawai`i Bar
	Works as a deputy attorney in the Office of the State Attorney General
1981-1994	Elected to Hawai`i House of Representatives from the 12th District, then the 20th District
August 8, 1989	Marries attorney Leighton Kim Oshima
1994 - 2002	Elected Lieutenant Governor; serves two terms
	Loses race for Hawai`i governor
2006 - 2013	Elected to U.S. House of Representatives; serves three two-year terms
2012	Elected to the U.S. Senate; is the first Asian American woman; only current immigrant in the Senate; only Buddhist; and Hawai`i's first woman elected to the U.S. Senate
2018	Re-elected to the U.S. Senate; serves on the Committee on the Judiciary, the Committee on Armed Services, and the Committee on Energy and Natural Resources, among others
March 19, 2021	Mother Laura passes away at age 96

ABOUT THE AUTHOR

Leslie Ann Hayashi is a retired judge, author, and artist. She has written several children's books, contributed to various short story collections, and won several writing awards. Her husband, Alan Van Etten, is an attorney in Honolulu. Both are proud members of the ABA since the 1970s and 1980s. Their older son, Justin, is in-house counsel at Figma in San Francisco. He and his wife, Jannie, have a daughter, Tanni, whom Gma and Gpa love dearly. Their second son, Taylor, works for Remitly in Seattle. He and his wife Marina are parents to a beautiful Corgi named Freya.

www.leslieahayashi.com

ABOUT THE ILLUSTRATOR

Tammy Yee is the author and/or illustrator of more than 40 children's books. She grew up in Hawai`i where she explored tide pools, swam in streams, and wrote and illustrated spooky stories her teachers politely read. After working as a pediatric medical-surgical and oncology nurse, in 1994 she exchanged her stethoscope for a paintbrush and has been writing and illustrating ever since. She has also designed digital murals for local health centers, pediatric hospitals, and ambulances. In 2022, she was inducted into the Children's Literature of Hawai`i's (CLH) Hall of Fame.

www.tammyyee.com